CH

I0426964

Learning About Earning

Cavendish Square
New York

Fran Hatton

Published in 2015 by Cavendish Square Publishing, LLC
243 5th Avenue, Suite 136, New York, NY 10016

CPSIA Compliance Information: Batch #WW15CSQ

All websites were available and accurate when this book was sent to press.

Library of Congress Cataloging-in-Publication Data

Hatton, Fran.
Learning about earning / Fran Hatton.
pages cm. — (First-glance finance)
Includes index.
ISBN 978-1-50260-094-3 (hardcover) ISBN 978-1-50260-102-5 (ebook)
1. Wages—Juvenile literature. 2. Labor—Juvenile literature. 3. Finance—Juvenile literature. I. Title.

HD4909.H3635 2015
331.2'1—dc23

2014026744

Editor: Amy Hayes
Senior Copy Editor: Wendy A. Reynolds
Art Director: Jeffrey Talbot
Senior Designer: Amy Greenan
Senior Production Manager: Jennifer Ryder-Talbot
Production Editor: David McNamara
Photo Research by J8 Media

Printed in the United States of America

CONTENTS

ONE / 4
The Early Days of Earning

TWO / 10
The Power of Earning

THREE / 16
How James Bought His Telescope

FOUR / 24
The Ups and Downs of Paychecks

FIVE / 29
How Do People Get Paid?

SIX / 35
Earning That Cash

GLOSSARY / 42

FIND OUT MORE / 45

INDEX / 46

ABOUT THE AUTHOR / 48

CHAPTER ONE

The Early Days of Earning

· ·

Thousands of years ago, after many years of being hunter-gatherers and nomads, our human ancestors started settling down. Instead of following herds of animals around or eating fruits and grains found in the wild, these people began farming crops and raising livestock. They became **producers**, and that changed their whole way of life.

Once people began to settle down, villages and towns sprung up, and with them came new economic

Early merchants would travel to distant ports to barter their wares.

opportunities. There is no written record of how these societies functioned, but there are artifacts and ruins that have been found and studied from all over the world. From the oldest archeological sites to the most recent, these discoveries share a common feature: **currency**.

The First Economy

These cultures were prehistoric, but we can speculate, or make an educated guess, about how money became important. In these long-gone villages, **barter** and trade was the first form of **economy**. Farmers would grow extra crops and then exchange them for tools, clothing, and other essentials. People began to see a demand for certain items and services, so the earliest professions included toolmaking, cloth making, and other types of production. The people who worked in these professions and traded their wares were the first skilled workers.

Beyond Barter

Eventually, however, the exchange of goods and services wasn't enough. What if the person who wove cloth didn't want to be paid in bags of wheat or barley? How many chickens would a blacksmith have to accept for a tool he had made? If merchants of any kind traveled a great distance to a market, how cumbersome would it be to make the return trip with profits made up of cotton bales? How were goods and services to be traded if everyone wanted the same thing?

Coins, such as these from the Chinese Tang Dynasty, have been used to represent currency for thousands of years.

The solution was currency. Civilizations and cultures created unified currencies, often using precious metals, either in raw form or made into coins. As people from different countries and regions came into contact with one another through trade, this currency changed hands. Gold and silver coins that were minted for one empire could be melted down again, refashioned, and still have value.

Workers that were paid in hard currency for their labor, rather than in exchange for something like room and board, could accumulate their earnings. They could now save and prosper. They could even carry their wealth with them, and perhaps move to a region where their **occupation** was more valued or there was more steady work to be found.

A Gold Standard

Over the past two millennia, societies have grown in fits and starts. There have been periods of stagnation, caused by the fall of empires, plagues, and so forth, but also periods of great growth. In the course of the development of modern civilization, countries have altered how money is made, in every respect.

Gold was once the most common measure of currency. Each dollar, euro, or yen was worth a certain amount of gold. In the last century, expensive wars took their toll on many cultures, and countries had to move away from this gold standard. Printed and coined money no longer has to be backed with its worth in

Gold is often used as a standard to set the value of currency.

gold. Some economists argue against this change, but the modern way makes working with great sums of money for things like federal budgets much easier.

It's been a long journey from the abacus to electronic bank transfers, but there is much in the way of earning money that remains the same. A basic understanding of earnings and wages will help you get where you want to be financially.

The First Calculators

In 1846 at an excavation site in Greece, archeologists unearthed an abacus that dates back to 3000 BCE. It is considered to be the oldest abacus ever found, and it proves that there has long been a need to calculate sums. There is much evidence to support that the first abacus originated in China in around 5000 BCE. In those ancient times, keeping track of the number of cattle someone owned, or how much meat cost per pound, was essential to doing business. The same was true for keeping track of **wages** paid and earned. These needs still exist today. However, our technology has improved a bit since 5000 BCE. Calculators now do most of the work for which abacuses once were used.

CHAPTER TWO

The Power of Earning

Money and More

It isn't hard to understand why people need to earn. In large part, it is because people spend. Sometimes they spend on necessities like food, housing, and utilities. Other times they spend money on entertainment, like going to a movie or buying something special. No matter the culture or currency, the old phrase "money makes the world go 'round" is an eternal truth. People strive to keep their jobs so that they have a continuous **income** to spend, save, and invest.

An income doesn't just provide for basic needs, it enables a more comfortable and enjoyable life for workers and their loved ones.

Earning isn't just about money, though. You can earn a variety of things. **Benefits**, discounts, and **career** education are some of the things you can earn as an **employee**. All of these different perks are considered **compensation**, even though they aren't specifically dollars and cents. Sometimes, these types of compensation are even more valuable than the money an employee earns.

How Much?

People from all walks of life find ways to earn. Waitresses, farmers, barbers, and lawyers all earn wages from their jobs. Most adults find that having a job that offers compensation is a priority. From plumbers to doctors, everyone who works gets paid.

However, different workers get paid different wages—generally, a doctor is paid more than a waitress. How do people determine how much compensation they deserve for their work? There are many factors in determining how a person gets paid, and how much.

Most items that have been manufactured, from cars to microwaves, have been built by workers with specialized skills.

Specialization

When a person **specializes** in something, it means that they become an expert in an area or acquire a particular skill. A job that is specialized can't just be done by someone off the street. It requires an expert. Similarly, a person who decides to specialize must put a lot of work, and sometimes money, into becoming qualified for that job.

Specialization leads to higher wages for several reasons. Many people would only spend the significant amount of time and money this training requires if they knew they were going to be rewarded. So a higher **salary** is there to motivate people to become specialized. However, few people are actually motivated enough to see the training through. This decreases the amount of qualified applicants for jobs, and **employers** have to compete for the specialized **professionals**, which they do by raising salaries.

Experience

People who have more experience at something usually get paid more, even if they are working the same job as another person. Why? The experience they gain from working in a particular position is often the most valuable asset an employee can have. As people continue to work in their jobs, they learn and improve. They become experts at their specific role. Often an increase in wages for employees with experience is a way of convincing these expert employees to stay with their employers. Sometimes employees who are especially good at their jobs are **promoted** and take on more responsibility, which usually means an increase in wages as well.

Living Off Interest

E ven folks who live off inherited wealth earn money through interest rates. Their base is a certain amount of money, which is called the **principal**, which they invest. As their investment grows, they live off of the money that is earned by the investments. They also try to never use any of the principal itself. By maintaining their principal balance, they know what they can expect to earn based on interest rates.

Salary vs. Hourly Pay

People get paid in different ways. For example, James is a babysitter who takes care of his younger cousin Isaac three times a week. Babysitting is an hourly job, which means that for every hour James works, he earns money. At the end of each week his aunt writes him a check. One week, his aunt got very sick, and James helped out by babysitting for five days that week. At the end of the week, his aunt was all better, and handed James a check. However, this check was for more money than

For many teenagers, babysitting is their first job.

the previous ones. James worked two more days, so he earned more money.

James talks to his mother about her job, and discovers she has a salary. Having a salary means a person will be paid a predetermined amount per year that will be divided equally over every paycheck. Sometimes James's mother works long hours, and sometimes she gets days off for holidays or vacations. However, every Friday his mother receives a check for the same amount. Her wage is not determined by the number of hours she works, but her overall value to her employers.

CHAPTER THREE

How James Bought His Telescope

Your First Job

Lots of people start their first job in middle school or high school. In fact, more than a quarter of the U.S. population of teenagers between the ages of sixteen and nineteen have a job.

Many first jobs aren't specialized or salaried. Some teenagers work their first jobs at a local restaurant, corner store, or library. Others work at summer camps, or even

The first cash you earn is always very exciting.

help out at sporting events. All of these first jobs have one thing in common: they are paid by the hour.

What's My Wage?

Remember James and his job babysitting his cousin? Once James realized he earned according to how much he worked, he knew that he could figure out how much he earned for each hour.

James received a check for $54.00. He knows that he worked 3 days for 2 hours each day.

James figured out his hourly wage by looking at the check his aunt gave him.

$$\begin{array}{r} 3 \text{ days} \\ \times\ 2 \text{ hours} \\ \hline 6 \text{ hours total} \end{array}$$

James worked a total of six hours this week. To find out how much he earned per hour, James needs to divide the total amount he was paid by the number of hours he worked.

how much James earned per hour

number of hours James worked →

$$6\overline{\smash{\big)}\,\begin{array}{r}9.00\\54.00\\-54\\\hline 0\end{array}}$$

total amount James was paid

James learns that he earns $9.00 each hour he babysits. That is great news! James now has an income, or regular wage, and he has ideas on how to spend it.

Taking It All into Account

Each school day, James has to buy his lunch, which costs $1.50. The $1.50 spent on lunch money is an **expense**, which means it will be taken out of his profits.

The money left over from his babysitting income can be used for other things like snacks, or going to the movies with friends.

However, James has been eyeing a new telescope in the front window of a shop he walks by on the way home from school. James knows the telescope is $200.00. He wants to find out how long it will take him to save up to buy it. So, the first thing James does is figure out his work schedule. He takes out his planner and looks at the calendar section. He and his aunt have written out a schedule of each day that James has planned to babysit his cousin. It looks like this:

APRIL

SUN	MON	TUE	WED	THU	FRI	SAT
	Babysitting: 3–5pm	Babysitting: 3–5pm		Babysitting: 3–5pm		
	Babysitting: 3–5pm		Babysitting: 3–5pm		Babysitting: 5–9pm	
	Babysitting: 3–5pm	Babysitting: 3–5pm		Babysitting: 3–5pm		
	Babysitting: 3–5pm	Babysitting: 3–5pm	Babysitting: 3–5pm	Babysitting: 3–5pm		

James tallies up the hours that he will work for the month. If James babysits Isaac each day he is scheduled to, he will work 28 hours in the month of April. He decides

Make Your Own
Work Schedule

When people start a job, they are given a work schedule, which tells them when they will be working. You can use a planner or calendar to make your own work schedule. Take out your planner and a pencil and write down every chore you have to do. For example, if you have to take the garbage out every Tuesday night, you would write that down on each Tuesday. This will help you stay organized and show you how much work you have to do. Once you've finished, take a look at your schedule. If you think you can do more, talk to your parents or guardians. If you start doing more chores, they might raise your allowance.

to total up how much he will make in the coming month. James multiplies the hours he works by the pay he makes per hour:

$$28 \text{ hours}$$
$$\times \ \$9.00/\text{hour}$$
$$\overline{\$252.00 \text{ total}}$$

James's **expected income**, or wages he thinks he will make for the month of April, is $252.00. At first, James believes this will be more than enough to buy his telescope. Then he remembers that he will have to buy lunch at school. The money James will spend to buy lunch each day will take a chunk out of the money he wants to use to buy the telescope. In order to really find out when James will be able to afford to buy the telescope, James has to factor in his lunch expense. To do this, he first figures out how many lunches he has to buy. He knows he goes to school five days of the week, and that there are four weeks in April. So he multiplies:

$$5 \text{ days}$$
$$\times \ 4 \text{ weeks}$$
$$\overline{20 \text{ days}}$$

James will have to buy lunch for twenty days. Next, he multiplies the cost of the lunch by the number of lunches he will have to buy:

$$
\begin{array}{r}
\$1.50 \\
\times \quad 20 \\
\hline
\$30.00
\end{array}
$$

James will have to pay $30.00 for lunch this month. Finally, James can figure out if he can afford to by a new telescope by subtracting his lunch expenses from his expected income:

$$
\begin{array}{r}
\$252.00 \\
- \quad \$30.00 \\
\hline
\$222.00
\end{array}
$$

$252.00 — expected income
$30.00 — lunch expenses
$222.00 — profit

James will have enough money to buy the $200.00 telescope, and he even has some money left over in case he has an unexpected expense, such as replacing a phone charger or going out with friends.

The Power of Earning

Because James took the time to learn what he earned, he was able to plan and buy something pretty expensive. Earning an income from an hourly wage is

With careful planning and knowing how much you earn, you can make a big purchase just like James.

a great way to start learning about how work you do translates into value.

How do you think you should take control of what you earn? If you get an allowance, you might be able to plan out your expected income like James did. If you get money for doing chores or getting good grades, you can learn more about how much you get paid for each task.

CHAPTER FOUR

The Ups and Downs of Paychecks

What's It Worth to You?

The initial reaction when someone asks you how much money you want to earn may be, "As much as I can!" Everyone would like to make a lot of money, or at least have a lot of money. However, no one ever said making money was easy. Sometimes the path to a high-paying job is difficult to navigate. Other times, it may seem as if you work hard, yet you don't make as much as you'd like.

Keep working and you will be surprised how your money piles up.

Thinking things through is an important process, and will save you time and frustration in the long run. What do you want to earn? Successful people think about more than just how much they will get paid. They have to consider all they will gain in exchange for what they will be doing to earn it.

Before Your First Paycheck

Many people work very hard and spend a lot of money before they ever receive their first paycheck, just to get a job. As mentioned before, if you want to specialize in something it takes a lot of work. There are a lot of good things about becoming a specialized worker. For one thing, there is a good chance you will get hired for the job you have trained for. For another, you will probably earn more than someone in a nonspecialized profession.

However, becoming specialized can be very difficult. It takes a lot of training and education, and paying for college is very expensive, though the cost can go down if

It can take years of study and hard work before you get your first specialized job, but the rewards of a career are worth it.

you do well in school and get a scholarship. It also is a lot of work, almost like a job itself. Finally there is the time required. It takes four years to earn a bachelor's degree, and even more for a master's or doctorate. While you might be training for your future career, other people are out working and earning money.

Some specializations do allow you to earn money while you learn. If you decide to become an electrician, for example, you need to start an **apprenticeship**. During an apprenticeship, you work closely with a trained expert in the field and get paid at a reduced rate to learn as you work. Another way to get trained and sometimes get paid is to have an **internship**. Many interns aren't paid any money, but they do earn a lot. Interns gain experience, learn on the job, and meet people who might help them get a job down the road.

Is It Worth It?

Sometimes a job might pay well, but it doesn't make you happy. Perhaps you find the work you're doing boring, or the environment you work in makes you upset. Maybe you don't think the work you're paid to do is good for the community.

All of these are reasons why some people don't enjoy working at their jobs. It is important that you as a worker feel respected by your coworkers, and valued as an employee. A job with a lower paycheck but with a better environment might be worth the change.

Clocking In

Another important factor when considering earning is what you will be giving up to work. You are not only trading your talents, you are giving up your time. How many hours do you think is okay to spend working? What might you miss out on if your job demands you to work every day?

A smart way to make sure you aren't working too much is to weigh your other responsibilities, including schoolwork, friends, and family, against the amount of time at a job. Adults do this all the time. Sometimes a parent decides that taking care of a child is more important than working at a job outside of the house, and will work fewer hours or quit their job to be a parent. Other times adults know they need to earn more than they do, and consider getting a second job to help with bills.

Job Versus Career: What's the Difference?

Careers are fulfilling and exciting, but it can take a lot of work to have one.

A job is a contract between you and your employer. You will work in exchange for money. A career is much more than that. Think about when you were little and people asked what you wanted to do when you grow up. Did you want to be a doctor, or a teacher, or an astronaut? A career is kind of like a dream job. It is a job that will be exciting and fulfilling. A career is a goal you set for yourself, because in many cases, you have to train very hard to have a career. If you want to be a ballerina, you have to practice dancing every day. If you want to be a veterinarian, you have to study biology for years. Careers are rewarding, and often pay higher wages than jobs.

CHAPTER FIVE

How Do People Get Paid?

....

Have you talked to your parent or guardian about how they earn? Learning about the best way to earn money may seem like something you won't need to know until you grow up, but the way your parents and guardians earn wages is actually affecting you today. Being aware of the different ways people earn can help prepare you for a successful career.

Hourly Wage

Your first job might be a minimum wage, hourly position. There is a federal minimum wage, a standard amount that is the least amount an employer can legally pay an

Minimum Wage
State to State

employee, but each state determines its own rate. You can find out your state's minimum wage by contacting the state legislature, or by asking employers in your area.

The good and the bad part of hourly wages is that you get paid for exactly how much time you work. Think back to James and his babysitting job. It is pretty great that James got a bigger check for helping out when his aunt was sick. However, James's aunt is a teacher, so she doesn't need James to babysit during the summer. Suddenly, James's income disappears, and he makes nothing. Hourly wages are not the most dependable, and they can fluctuate a lot from month to month.

Working as a clerk in a grocery store is a common first job and often pays minimum wage.

Commission

Another way lots of people get paid is by **commission**. Realtors and some salespeople earn commission for everything that they sell. The money a realtor gets for selling a house is supposed to motivate him or her to be as successful as possible. Those who are particularly good salespeople can make a lot of money through commission.

However, there is a downside to this kind of earning. Usually your base pay is not very high. This means if you have a slow week and nobody buys anything from you,

Realtors, who help people buy and sell houses, will earn money based on the price of the house—this percentage is known as a commission.

you can come home with a very small check. Like hourly wages, commission wages can vary depending on the economy, or the time of year.

Salary

James's mom works at a salaried position. This means that no matter how many hours she works at the office, once a week she receives a check for the same amount every time. Initially, you might think this is unfair. Shouldn't people get paid for the amount they work? However, this system is very helpful for both the employer and employee.

For example, James's mom has to work late for a few days in November, which means that she gets paid less per hour than she normally would. That may seem unfair, but she also gets the Thursday and Friday of Thanksgiving off—and even though she only worked three days that week, she still gets a check for the same amount as a five-day week. If she had worked an hourly wage job, she might be scrambling to make ends meet, but instead, she is secure because she has a salaried position. Salaries are also nice for planning payments in the future because you know how much money you will make each year. Adults can more easily decide whether or not they can afford a house or a new car than if the amount of money coming in fluctuates.

Benefits

Benefits such as vacation time are another important part of earning.

Salaried jobs usually come with benefits, but some hourly and commission jobs offer them as well. Benefits are a part of what you earn. Even though they aren't cash, they can add up. Some benefits include employee health insurance, investment plans, life insurance, pensions, sick days, personal days, and vacation time. This might sound pretty boring, but they

What Is a 401(k), Anyway?

A 401(k) plan is a way to save for retirement. Employees have their employers take money out of their paycheck and set it aside to grow in a special fund. Some employers will even contribute a bit of their own money to your fund. This is called a match. It's like saving twice the money you put in!

are often the most important part of what people earn. Benefits can make or break your finances. If you get sick, having insurance to go to the hospital means you do not have to spend your own savings to get well. Having sick time means you still get paid for the day you miss at work. Employers even offer workplace learning, where employees can take courses for free. Most people try to plan out their careers so that they have jobs with good benefit plans.

CHAPTER SIX

Earning That Cash

· ·

Now that you've gained an idea of what it means to earn an income, it's time to get to work! With each type of job you have, there are important considerations you need to think about in order achieve long-term success. Being confident and learning about what you earn will help you now, and in the future.

Remember that there are many different ways to get paid, not just in cash. Think about the career you want. What steps do you need to take to achieve your dream job? What experiences do you have or need to gain? Maybe you're not old enough to start working

Take pride and find satisfaction with the work you do and the money you earn.

a traditional first job at a fast-food restaurant or a summer camp. However, it is good to understand the opportunities that you do have available.

Understanding Opportunity

If you know that you want to earn a salary, remember that you will have to work hard to specialize. If the job you want requires a college degree, try to look at your homework as an opportunity to earn good grades and learn. Many other opportunities exist as well. Taking care of a family member or volunteering is a great way to earn experience and gain connections that might help you get a paying job in the future.

But I Need It Now!

What can you do about earning money today? If you do get an allowance, talk to your parents or guardians about what you earn. Ask how you earn your allowance money. Do you do chores, or help out around the house? Maybe your parents give you an allowance as a learning tool. Ask your parent or guardian if there are things they would be willing to pay you for, like mowing the lawn or washing the floors.

Once you have decided what job to take on, discuss with them what a good rate would be for the value you would provide. Decide whether or not you should be paid hourly for your time or weekly if it's something you have to do on a regular basis. For example, if you decide to help by washing the car, that is something that you would probably want to be paid hourly for, since it is a once-in-a-while chore. If you decide to mow the lawn, you would have to do that more often, perhaps even weekly, so a salary might make more sense for the summertime. If you address your new responsibilities and your wages seriously, you may get a good rate for your work, a steady job doing some extra chores, and more cash!

Your parents can help you take the money you earn and put it into a bank account.

Learning about Earning

Direct Deposit

Depending on the company you work for, you may be able to get your paychecks sent directly to your bank account through direct deposit. There are several advantages to this. First, you often receive your money in your account faster. Second, you don't have to make a trip to the bank each time you get a paycheck.

Payday!

Once you have your first payday, it's time to open a bank account. The two main types of accounts are savings and checking. With your parent's help, shop around at the different banks in your town. They may offer different kinds of accounts, particularly for students. There are many accounts that are customized just for people under the age of eighteen. If you can find a savings account that pays you interest on the money in your account, you can start earning more money on what you've already earned. Some accounts do charge monthly fees, so make sure to do some research before you decide what kind of account you want.

Framed
First Buck

The next time you go into an independently owned store or a mom-and-pop diner, look for something special. Many people who start their own small businesses keep and frame the first dollar bill they earn when the establishment opens. Financial success for them, as for most of us, begins with hard effort and is measured in small steps forward.

You don't have to put all your earnings into savings—it can be fun to have some "walking around money" in case you see something you'd like to buy.

A Look Back

It's amazing how far civilization has come from bartering chickens for wool. People earn in all different sorts of ways now, and money changes hands easier than ever before. With the advances in technology, from the telegraph to the Internet, there have been changes in how money is stored in banks and transferred. Even aspects of work, such as logging hours and receiving payment, have become electronic in some way or another. Many companies insist on using direct deposit, a system that allows employers to send their employees' earnings right into their private bank accounts.

Moving Forward

Now that you understand what people earn and how they are paid for their work, you are equipped to start finding your first job, and earning your first wage. Whatever you do as you move forward, remember that earning can be about more than just money.

apprenticeship A person who learns a job or skill by working for a fixed period of time for an expert.

barter To trade one thing for another without the use of money.

benefit A service (such as health insurance) or right (such as taking vacation time) provided by an employer in addition to wages or salary.

career A job or profession someone does for a long time.

commission An amount of money paid to an employee for selling something.

compensation Payment for doing a job.

currency Another word for money.

employee A person who works for an individual or company, in return for pay.

employer An individual or business that pays someone for their skills or service.

expected income The amount an employee believes they will earn.

expense Money spent on something.

internship An opportunity for a student or recent graduate to work for a period of time in order to gain experience.

occupation A specific task or job.

principal An amount of money that is invested in order to earn interest.

GLOSSARY

producer Someone who makes items for sale.

professional Relating to work that requires skill or education.

promoted To have received a job with more responsibility and higher pay.

salary Income paid on a regular, scheduled basis.

specialize To become an expert at something.

wages Money you earn.

Books

Hunter, Nick. *Earning Money*. Mankato, MN: Heinemann InfoSearch, 2011.

Vernon, Naomi. *A Teen's Guide to Finding a Job*. Seattle, WA: Amazon Digital Services, 2014.

Wilkes, Donald L., and Hamilton-Wilkes, Viola. *Teen Guide Job Search*. Lincoln, NE: iUniverse, 2007.

Websites

Earning
www.themint.org/kids/ways-kids-can-earn-money.html
Check out the ways to earn money and see if you can be your own boss at TheMint.org.

Financial Entertainment
financialentertainment.org
This site has a variety of interactive games that cover many different concepts, including how to earn.

Making Money
pbskids.org/itsmylife/money/making
This PBS Kids GO! webpage gives great suggestions on how to earn money at any age.

INDEX

Page numbers in
boldface
are illustrations.

401(k), 34

abacus, 8–9
allowance, 20, 23, 37
apprenticeship, 26

babysitting, 14, **15**, 17,
  19, 30
bank accounts
  checking, 39
  direct deposit, 39, 41
  fees, 39
  researching, 39
  savings, 34, 39, **41**
barter, 5–6, **5**, 41

benefits, 11, 33–34, **33**
  health insurance, 33
  investment plans, 33
  pensions, 33
  personal days, 33
  sick days, 33
  vacation, 15, 33, **33**

career, 11, 26, **26**, 28–29,
  28, 34–35
chores, 20, 23, 37
commission, 31–33, **32**
  base pay, 31
compensation, 11–12
currency, 5, **6**, 7, **8**, 10

economist, 8
employee, 11, 13, 27, 30,
    32–34, 41
employer, 13, 15, 28–30,
    32, 34, 41
expected income,
    21–23, 34
expense, 18, 21–22

first job, **15**, 16–17, 29,
    31, 36, 41

gold standard, 7

hourly pay, 14
    See also income; wages

income, 10, **11**, 18–19, 22,
    30, 35
internship, 26

minimum wage, 29–30, 31

occupation, 7

payday, 39
paycheck, 15, 25, 27, 34, 39
principal, 14
producer, 4
professional, 13
profit, 6, 18, 22
promoted, 13

realtors, 31, **32**
retirement, 34

salary, 13, 15, 36–37
silver, 7
specialize, 12–13, **12**, 25, 36
    job, 16, **26**
    professional, 13
    worker, 25

wages, 8–9, 11–13, 21,
    28–30, 32, 37
workplace learning, 34
work schedule, 19–20

Fran Hatton is a freelance author and editor who has spent her entire career working with the printed word in one form or another. She has written several books for Cavendish Square, including another in the First-Glance Finance series, *Starting a Business*. Her husband and children bring her more joy than all the books in the world, and nothing can compete with that. PA native of Indiana, Ms. Hatton now resides in Orlando, Florida.